FRANCIS FRITH'S
PHOTOGRAPHIC MEMORIES

NORTHWICH

JIM RUBERY has lived in Yorkshire since 1975, having moved to the south of the county after being educated in the Midlands. He is a very keen participant in outdoor pursuits, and has spent a great deal of his spare time over the years climbing, mountaineering, walking, skiing, and canoeing, and has even dabbled with caving and sailing. He started writing for the climbing press in the early 1990s, and he has had a regular walking column in Cheshire Life magazine since 1997, entitled 'Rambling with Rubery'. This is also now a regular monthly feature in the sister magazines Yorkshire Life and Lancashire Life. Wherever possible, Jim tries to incorporate a place of interest along the way in his walks, often a historic building or area of archaeological importance. It is from this that his love of historical places has grown, whether it is a prehistoric stone circle, a ruined castle or abbey from medieval times or a relatively modern building from the Industrial Revolution. Over the past six years, Jim has spent many happy hours walking the footpaths and bridleways of Cheshire, enjoying its lovely countryside and exploring its quaint villages and towns; Northwich is a particular favourite.

FRANCIS FRITH'S
PHOTOGRAPHIC MEMORIES

NORTHWICH

PHOTOGRAPHIC MEMORIES

JIM RUBERY

First published in the United Kingdom in 2003 by
Frith Book Company Ltd

Paperback Edition 2003
ISBN 1-85937-677-0

British Library Cataloguing in Publication Data

Francis Frith's Northwich
Jim Rubery

Frith Book Company Ltd
Frith's Barn, Teffont,
Salisbury, Wiltshire SP3 5QP
Tel: +44 (0) 1722 716 376
Email: info@francisfrith.co.uk
www.francisfrith.co.uk

Printed and bound in Great Britain

Front Cover: NORTHWICH, *Swing Bridge 1900* 45422

Frontispiece: NORTHWICH, *The River from Winnington Bridge c1955* N43022

CONTENTS

FRANCIS FRITH
VICTORIAN PIONEER

FRANCIS FRITH, founder of the world-famous photographic archive, was a complex and multi-talented man. A devout Quaker and a highly successful Victorian businessman, he was philosophic by nature and pioneering in outlook.

By 1855 he had already established a wholesale grocery business in Liverpool, and sold it for the astonishing sum of £200,000, which is the equivalent today of over £15,000,000. Now a very rich man, he was able to indulge his passion for travel. As a child he had pored over travel books written by early explorers, and his fancy and imagination had been stirred by family holidays to the sublime mountain regions of Wales and Scotland. 'What lands of spirit-stirring and enriching scenes and places!' he had written. He was to return to these scenes of grandeur in later years to 'recapture the thousands of vivid and tender memories', but with a different purpose. Now in his thirties, and captivated by the new science of photography, Frith set out on a series of pioneering journeys up the Nile and to the

Near East that occupied him from 1856 until 1860.

INTRIGUE AND EXPLORATION

These far-flung journeys were packed with intrigue and adventure. In his life story, written when he was sixty-three, Frith tells of being held captive by bandits, and of fighting 'an awful midnight battle to the very point of surrender with a deadly pack of hungry, wild dogs'. Wearing flowing Arab costume, Frith arrived at Akaba by camel seventy years before Lawrence of Arabia, where he encountered 'desert princes and rival sheikhs, blazing with jewel-hilted swords'.

He was the first photographer to venture beyond the sixth cataract of the Nile. Africa was still the mysterious 'Dark Continent', and Stanley and Livingstone's historic meeting was a decade into the future. The conditions for picture taking confound belief. He laboured for hours in his wicker dark-room in the sweltering heat of the desert, while the volatile chemicals fizzed dangerously in their trays. Back in London he exhibited his photographs and was 'rapturously cheered' by members of the Royal Society. His reputation as a photographer was made overnight.

VENTURE OF A LIFE-TIME

Characteristically, Frith quickly spotted the opportunity to create a new business as a specialist publisher of photographs. He lived in an era of immense and sometimes violent change.

For the poor in the early part of Victoria's reign work was exhausting and the hours long, and people had precious little free time to enjoy themselves. Most had no transport other than a cart or gig at their disposal, and rarely travelled far beyond the boundaries of their own town or village. However, by the 1870s the railways had threaded their way across the country, and Bank Holidays and half-day Saturdays had been made obligatory by Act of Parliament. All of a sudden the working man and his family were able to enjoy days out and see a little more of the world.

With typical business acumen, Francis Frith foresaw that these new tourists would enjoy having souvenirs to commemorate their days out. In 1860 he married Mary Ann Rosling and set out on a new career: his aim was to photograph every city, town and village in Britain. For the next thirty years he travelled the country by train and by pony and trap, producing fine photographs of seaside resorts and beauty spots that were keenly bought by millions of Victorians. These prints were painstakingly pasted into family albums and pored over during the dark nights of winter, rekindling precious memories of summer excursions.

THE RISE OF FRITH & CO

Frith's studio was soon supplying retail shops all over the country. To meet the demand he gath-

ered about him a small team of photographers, and published the work of independent artist-photographers of the calibre of Roger Fenton and Francis Bedford. In order to gain some understanding of the scale of Frith's business one only has to look at the catalogue issued by Frith & Co in 1886: it runs to some 670 pages, listing not only many thousands of views of the British Isles but also many photographs of most European countries, and China, Japan, the USA and Canada - note the sample page shown on page 9 from the hand-written Frith & Co ledgers recording the pictures. By 1890 Frith had created the greatest specialist photographic publishing company in the world, with over 2,000 sales outlets - more than the combined number that Boots and WH Smith have today! The picture on the next page shows the Frith & Co display board at Ingleton in the Yorkshire Dales (left of window). Beautifully constructed with a mahogany frame and gilt inserts, it could display up to a dozen local scenes.

POSTCARD BONANZA

The ever-popular holiday postcard we know today took many years to develop. In 1870 the Post Office issued the first plain cards, with a pre-printed stamp on one face. In 1894 they allowed other publishers' cards to be sent through the mail with an attached adhesive half-penny stamp. Demand grew rapidly, and in 1895 a new size of postcard was permitted called the court card, but there was little room for illustration. In 1899, a year after Frith's death, a new card measuring 5.5 x 3.5 inches became the standard format, but it was not until 1902 that the divided back came into being, so that the address and message could be on one face and a full-size illustration on the other. Frith & Co were in the vanguard of postcard development: Frith's sons Eustace and Cyril continued their father's monumental task, expanding the number of views offered to the public and recording more

and more places in Britain, as the coasts and countryside were opened up to mass travel.

Francis Frith had died in 1898 at his villa in Cannes, his great project still growing. The archive he created continued in business for another seventy years. By 1970 it contained over a third of a million pictures showing 7,000 British towns and villages.

FRANCIS FRITH'S LEGACY

Frith's legacy to us today is of immense significance and value, for the magnificent archive of evocative photographs he created provides a unique record of change in the cities, towns and villages throughout Britain over a century and more. Frith and his fellow studio photographers revisited locations many times down the years to update their views, compiling for us an enthralling and colourful pageant of British life and character.

We are fortunate that Frith was dedicated to recording the minutiae of everyday life. For it is this sheer wealth of visual data, the painstaking chronicle of changes in dress, transport, street layouts, buildings, housing, engineering and landscape that captivates us so much today. His remarkable images offer us a powerful link with the past and with the lives of our ancestors.

THE VALUE OF THE ARCHIVE TODAY

Computers have now made it possible for Frith's many thousands of images to be accessed almost instantly. Frith's images are increasingly used as visual resources, by social historians, by researchers into genealogy and ancestry, by architects and town planners, and by teachers involved in local history projects.

In addition, the archive offers every one of us an opportunity to examine the places where we and our families have lived and worked down the years. Highly successful in Frith's own era, the archive is now, a century and more on, entering a new phase of popularity. Historians consider the Francis Frith Collection to be of prime national importance. It is the only archive of its kind remaining in private ownership. Francis Frith's archive is now housed in an historic timber barn in the beautiful village of Teffont in Wiltshire. Its founder would not recognize the archive office as it is today. In place of the many thousands of dusty boxes containing glass plate negatives and an all-pervading odour of photographic chemicals, there are now ranks of computer screens. He would be amazed to watch his images travelling round the world at unimaginable speeds through internet lines.

The archive's future is both bright and exciting. Francis Frith, with his unshakeable belief in making photographs available to the greatest number of people, would undoubtedly approve of what is being done today with his lifetime's work. His photographs depicting our shared past are now bringing pleasure and enlightenment to millions around the world a century and more after his death.

NORTHWICH
SALT OF THE EARTH

Northwich is a town that has quite literally, as well as metaphorically, been built upon salt, with thick rock salt seams and natural brine streams underlying much of the land in the region. It was one of the three original 'wiches', or salt towns - the others were Nantwich and Middlewich. The salt was laid down 255-190 million years ago, during the Triassic Period, when a shallow, tropical sea covered the area.

Salt has always been a valuable commodity; it was used initially as a food preservative, but later for chemical and manufacturing industries. It is known that from around 70AD the Romans first collected brine from naturally occurring brine springs that surfaced along the banks of the River Weaver. Salt making was probably started during this period under military supervision, and four lead salt pans, with cast inscriptions (which have been dated to this time) have been found in the area.

BARNTON, *The Tunnel c1955* B518006

Natural brine is made when groundwater dissolves the rock salt and then flows as brine streams that sporadically erupt at the surface with very high salt concentrations. The brine can then be collected, the water evaporated off and salt crystals produced. For an in-depth history of salt in Northwich, the Salt Museum on London Road is completely devoted to an explanation and interpretation of the salt industry, and is a must for any local or visitor to the region. It is based in Weaver Hall, which was built as a workhouse in 1837.

Roman Northwich

Although a few stone tools and flint knaps have been found in and around Northwich and Vale Royal, showing that prehistoric farmers were in the area some 5,000 years ago, it was the Romans, around 70AD, who first settled here. They built a timber auxiliary fort, which they called Condate, on Castle Hill, close to the point where the Rivers Dane and Weaver join and where the military road between Chester and Manchester crossed the Weaver. The name 'Condate', meaning 'confluence', may also indicate the worship of the Celtic god Condatis, the guardian of waters meeting, as it was customary to pray to the water spirits before crossing.

Northwich, Middlewich and Wilderspool served as supply bases for the Roman military to the north. A variety of industrial processes have been identified from this period of occupation, including several furnaces, smithing hearths, and a potting kiln operated by a person who stamped the name 'Maco' on his wares. In fact, so industrious was this part of Cheshire at the time that it has been referred to as the Roman Black Country.

The Middle Ages

By the time of the Domesday Survey in 1086, the salt industry at Northwich was well developed; it was valued at the considerable sum of £8 a year. The salt workers lived alongside the line of the old Roman road in Witton. The Manor of Northwich was recorded as an area of just 8 acres at the confluence of the Rivers Dane and Weaver, and belonging to the Earls of Chester. In 1255 Northwich was given to Edward, son of Henry III. Along with the Earldom of Chester, it remained in the possession of the monarch's eldest son until 1584, when Richard III gave it to Thomas Stanley (later Lord Derby).

During the Middle Ages salt, being an indispensable necessity of life, was fundamental to the prosperity of the town, and the salt making process was highly organised and regulated. Historically, Northwich was a very small settlement; but in 1588, William Smith describes it as being 'a proper town, having every Friday a market and yearly two fairs'. Its growth was reliant on several interconnecting factors. Firstly, its geographical position, in the very heart of the county, where trade routes from east and west and north and south intersect, meant that it was developing into a very busy thoroughfare. Secondly, it was often used as the location for Quarter Sessions to be held, and where the chief governors of the county and their entourage met. Thirdly, it was now a manor held by the very powerful and wealthy Earls of Derby; and lastly, but not least, its very important salt industry ensured the town's growth.

Into the 18th Century

In 1670, workmen prospecting for coal at nearby Marbury happened upon rock salt, a discovery that not only rocketed Northwich to the forefront of salt production and made it one of the leading forces in the Industrial Revolution, but dealt a considerable blow to the rival salt industries at Nantwich and Middlewich.

Changes in the method of salt extraction occurred at this time too, with deep mining and the small lead pans being replaced by larger iron pans which could be heated by coal in order to evaporate the water quickly. After 1779, new borings revealed that even deeper saltbeds existed, and extended over a much wider area than had been previously thought. These new lower beds, at about 175ft deep, were up to 12ft thick and of exceptional quality. With the sinking of deeper mines in 1781, salt production from 23 local salt mines increased dramatically from about 15,000 tons per year in the middle of the century to over 100,000 tons at its end.

The Weaver Navigation

The River Weaver has played an important role in the development of the salt industry in Northwich. Prior to 1721, it was a shallow waterway that flowed serenely from its source in the Peckforton Hills through the settlements of Wrenbury, Audlem, Nantwich, Winsford, Northwich and finally Frodsham, before pouring into the saline waters of the River Mersey. The Weaver has been used to move salt away from Cheshire for centuries, but only along its lower tidal reaches. Salt was brought down to the river on pack-horses to meet the oncoming tide, and sailing barges would load at high water and depart for Liverpool and other ports on the ebbing tide. This was a very labour intensive and unsatisfactory method, not helped by ever-

changing tide heights and times; so, in 1721, an Act of Parliament was granted to make the river a navigation from Frodsham through Northwich to Winsford, some 20 miles inland.

By 1732 the course of the river had been straightened out, the channel deepened and a series of locks built that could accommodate cargo boats of 100 tons. Northwich became an inland port, and boat yards sprang up along the river frontage with a wide variety of river and coastal vessels being constructed; these included 'Weaver flats', flat-bottomed sailing barges.

The Anderton Boat Lift

When the Trent and Mersey canal was built in 1777, the trustees of the Weaver Navigation were understandably very alarmed at the prospect of losing trade to the new waterway, but in the event the opposite occurred, and trade along the Navigation increased. At Anderton, the canal and the river ran parallel to each other, with the canal being just 50ft above the river. By 1800 a physical link had been established between the two waterways, which consisted of a series of chutes; these allowed salt to be tipped from barges on the canal into Weaver flats on the river below.

This system continued until 1875, when the great Anderton Boat Lift, known as 'the wonder of the waterways', was constructed. Edward Leader Williams, the Trustees' engineer, suggested the idea of constructing a 'boat-carrying lift', and along with Edwin Clarke, a prominent civil engineer of the time, he produced a magnificent design that was not only unique but typified the Victorians' ingenuity and ability for novel engineering projects. Originally the lift operated on a hydraulic system, with two counter-balanced water-tight tanks raising and lowering boats between the two waterways. It was electrified in 1908 and the system modified so that the tanks could be operated independently. This system worked well until 1983, when severe corrosion of the main support legs forced British Waterways to shut the lift down. A renovation programme has recently taken place, and the lift is now back in full working order.

Subsidence

By the middle of the 19th century, in addition to a number of works producing salt by the evaporation process, the Northwich mines were producing almost 300,000 tons of salt each year. By 1887, Cheshire was producing 80 per cent of British output, and after coal and iron, salt was the third largest bulk export commodity. However, the fast-increasing output and the dangerous process of brine pumping led to large-scale subsidence throughout the saltfield. There has always been natural subsidence in the area, and several of the meres and flashes (lakes) are a result of this natural phenomenon, but the extraction of rock salt greatly accelerated the process.

Cavernous holes appeared in streets, cracks developed in roads and walls, some buildings began to tilt at crazy angles, and others simply began to sink below ground; some buildings just collapsed into a pile of rubble. Not only were the town's buildings at risk, but the salt workers too. In 1838 Ashton's Mine at Witton flooded, and seven men drowned when a rush of water through the subterranean galleries overwhelmed the men before they could reach the surface.

For many years the salt companies refused to accept liability for subsidence and the immense damage it was causing, but in 1891, the Brine Pumping (Compensation of Subsidence) Act was passed, and people who had suffered the consequences of subsidence were able to claim compensation.

The Chemical Industry

In 1873 John Brunner and Ludwig Mond came together and purchased the Winnington Hall estate; here they established a plant that produced soda ash from salt. After early teething problems the works flourished, and the site became a factory town with its own model village for the workers. Management lived up-wind of the works at Hartford.

In 1926 Brunner Mond merged with other companies to form ICI, the largest salt makers in what was then the British Empire. Today brine from the salt works is used to make a range of alkali products that are used in the glass, cosmetic, fabric, paper and pharmaceutical industries.

Black and White

As a result of the immense damage and destruction caused by subsidence, many of the old buildings in the town had to be pulled down. For a time, between the late 1800s and early 1900s, Northwich resembled a shanty town with shops and single-storey timber sheds filling in the gaps where buildings had disappeared. However, owing to new building regulations which insisted that any new developments be based on a light timber framework, the town slowly recovered, and fine black and white timber-framed, multi-storey buildings began to emerge, decorated with ornate carvings and plaster-work. This has given the town a very attractive 'olde-worlde' feel, particularly along the High Street; here, the Old Post Office, built in 1911, and the Brunner Public Library, rebuilt after subsidence damage in 1909, are particularly fine examples from this period.

Not only were many buildings demolished and replaced but several were jacked up, particularly during the 'big-lift' of 1920-24 when the Bull Ring was also raised by 6ft in the battle against subsidence. The only building in Northwich to remain unaffected by subsidence was the Parish Church, thanks mainly to its unusual location some distance away from the town centre.

During the 1960's, much of the present town centre was redeveloped in order to make it a pedestrian zone and a number of old buildings demolished, including the Market Hall, Police Station and several pubs.

CASTLE STREET *c1965* N43077

THE STREETS OF NORTHWICH

THE SIR JOHN BRUNNER LIBRARY *c1955* N43007

This building was constructed in 1909 to replace an earlier one, built in 1886, which had to be demolished owing to subsidence. It was donated to the town by Sir John Brunner of Brunner Mond fame (the company was later to become ICI). Note the lack of security on the bicycles and pram outside the library - a sign of the times!

THE PUBLIC LIBRARY AND SALT MUSEUM
c1965 N43069

This shows the Sir John Brunner Library when it also served as the salt museum, before the latter was moved to Weaver Hall, formerly Northwich Workhouse, in London Road. Note the extensive use of timber in the building, which was designed to withstand stress caused by further subsidence. The street is now pedestrian only.

WITTON STREET *1903* 49670

This photograph was taken in the great pre-supermarket and convenience store days when each shop traded in its own specific wares. The shops nearest to us are selling boots and shoes. This photograph shows Witton Street before electric lighting was installed and before the cobbles were covered with tarmac. The clock hangs outside a jeweller's shop.

HIGH STREET
1903 49671

This shows the High Street, looking towards the Bull Ring, before the 'big-lift' of 1920-24 when the roads were raised, and the buildings either demolished and replaced or jacked up in the battle against subsidence. Notice the general lack of timber work in the buildings compared with today.

HIGH STREET *c1965* N43065

During the 1920s many of the buildings in Northwich were replaced or modified using timber-framed construction methods with ornate carvings and plasterwork. This has given the town a very attractive 'olde-worlde' feel, particularly along the High Street, which is now the start of the pedestrianised area.

THE BULL RING
1903 49678

Here we have a nostalgic scene at the very heart of old Northwich, at a time when tradesmen used horses and carts to transport their wares and tools around the streets. The Bull Ring was once the central meeting place and the hub of activity for the town. It was originally the location of a weekly market in the 17th century.

THE BULL RING *c1960* N43033

This photograph shows the Bull Ring some 60 years after No 49678. The attractive gas lamp has gone, to be replaced by an electrified concrete monstrosity; the street cobbles have been covered over with ubiquitous tarmac; and the Angel Hotel has been pulled down owing to subsidence. Technically, Northwich is the name given to the six-acre township surrounding the Bull Ring.

CARD CORNER *c1960* N43068

The photograph shows the High Street at its junction with Market Street. Note the four carved figures, very much like ship figureheads, on the buildings with dormer extensions to the roof (centre). The building to their left is the Midland Bank, built on the site of the 17th-century inn known as The Swan.

WITTON STREET
c1960 N43050

This area is technically Witton, one of the townships that make up the old settlement; the others are Winnington, Castle, Leftwich and Northwich. The large building on the left, the post office, is now a pub aptly called the Penny Black.

▶ **CASTLE STREET**
c1965 N43077

This photograph
shows Castle Street
from the bottom of
Verdin Park. In the
17th century there
were three or four
large mansions along
here with terraced
gardens behind – they
were the homes of
Northwich's well-off.

◀ **THE CROOKED
HOUSES**
1903 49673

Here we have an
outstanding example of
what subsidence could
do to a property. Pre-war
books describe
Northwich as a town
ravaged by the effects of
salt extraction, its streets
with doors and windows
twisted, walls riven with
cracks and whole
buildings leaning at
strange angles. This
house is thought to have
stood in London Road,
Leftwich.

▲ **THE COURT HOUSE** *c1965* N43066

New buildings which were constructed in Northwich had to be specially designed to withstand future subsidence due to salt extraction. The Court House is built around a steel girder frame that is set on separate foundations.

◄**OLD HOUSES**
1903 49674

This photograph shows a 17th-century thatched cottage being used as two shops, standing at the bottom of Winnington Hill. The notice pinned to the window of the right-hand cottage is advertising Thom's Soaps. The cottage itself looks as though it was in need of a good wash down.

THE OLD CURIOSITY SHOP

c1950 N43002

Here we see the same shop as in No 49674 many years later and now thatchless, at a time when it was known as Jo Allman's second-hand shop. It was full of all manner of bric-a-brac, with many of the more 'weather proof' items being stored on the pavement. Stories abound from that time of people alighting on valuable items amongst the piles of jumble.

THE ROBERT VERDIN MONUMENT *c1965* N43075

Robert Verdin was a dominant figure in the Cheshire salt trade in the 19th century; he ended his highly successful career as Liberal Member of Parliament for Northwich. Verdin was born in 1835, but died quite young on July 27 1887. There is a canon in front of the memorial which was captured during the Crimean War.

VERDIN PARK
1898 42142

Robert Verdin was an extremely successful businessman who became senior partner in the firm Joseph Verdin & Sons of Winsford, Northwich and Liverpool. He was also a local benefactor: he presented Northwich with a park and also its Brine Baths, a local health spa, which opened in 1887 – they are visible on the left of the photograph. An inscription on the building reads: 'Cleanliness is next to godliness'.

VIEW FROM VERDIN PARK *c1965* N43074

Living at The Brockhurst in Northwich, Robert Verdin was only too well aware of the problems that faced the town through salt mining. A Victorian traveller wrote of Northwich: 'One of the busiest and dirtiest towns in Cheshire.' The same writer continues: 'For there is an air of desolation and untidiness which one usually finds in a coal-mining district'.

▼ **VICTORIA INFIRMARY** *1898* 42141

This was established by Robert Verdin at the time of Queen Victoria's Golden Jubilee as part of a package – the park, the baths and the infirmary. The infirmary was originally one of Verdin's homes, when it was known as Winnington Bank House.

▶ **VICTORIA INFIRMARY** *c1955* N43029

This shows the entrance to the Victoria Infirmary at the top of Winnington Hill; a number of additional buildings have been added since photograph No 42141 was taken. The infirmary still serves the good people of Northwich today.

◀ SIR JOHN DEANE'S GRAMMAR SCHOOL
c1955 N43018

The school was originally established in 1557 by a local man, John Deane. The original school stood in the churchyard at Witton. A second building was built close by, and a third in Church Street. The present building, situated off London Road, Leftwich, is the fourth site for the school; it was opened in 1908, a gift from Sir John Brunner.

▶ THE BUS STATION
c1955 N43014

The bus station is now no longer at this location, which is now occupied by a KwikSave supermarket. The area behind the bus station was the home ground of Northwich Victoria Football Club.

THE REGION'S CHURCHES

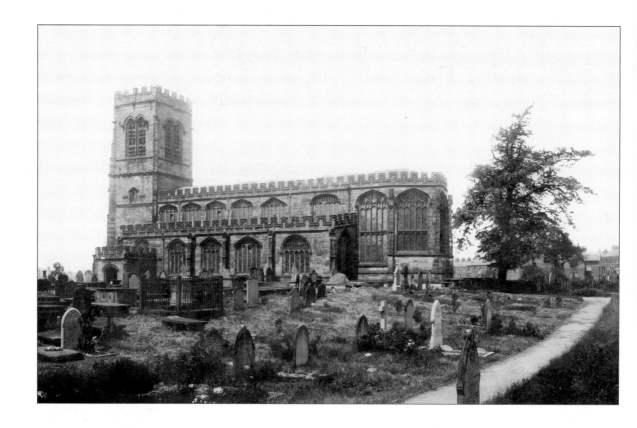

WITTON CHURCH *1898* 42139

St Helen's church is the oldest building in Northwich. This photograph shows the extensive use of windows in the construction of the church, effectively creating huge walls of glass that throw light into the church interior. Today, many of the headstones visible in the photograph have been removed, along with the metal railings surrounding the central tomb.

WITTON CHURCH
THE INTERIOR *1898* 42140

With buildings not only tilting at crazy angles, but also totally collapsing in Northwich owing to subsidence, we may be thankful that the church of St Helen has survived relatively unscathed. The interior of the building is spacious, and the vast eastern windows shed ample light into this ancient building. Part of the 19th-century restoration involved the rebuilding of the north arcade to create the wider nave. The nave and chancel roof, which date from 1525, are quite splendid, with superb panelling and carved bosses.

THE PARISH CHURCH *c1960* N43071

Although giving the impression of being Victorian, this visually impressive church is mainly in the Perpendicular style, having been built between 1498 and 1525, although it was heavily restored in the 1800s. One of the late additions to the church is a clock on each face of the tower, just below the bell louvres. When it was originally erected the church was in fact a chapel of ease - the mother church was Great Budworth.

HOLY TRINITY CHURCH *1903* 49676

The trustees of the Weaver Navigation used some of the profits that accrued from the dues that they charged to finance certain good works. One example was the construction of churches, such as this neat building in the Gothic style on Castle Street, built in 1842. The idea was to provide a place of worship for the watermen and their families on Sundays.

ST PAUL'S CHURCH
1903 49677

St Paul's church on London Road, near to Dane Bridge, was built in 1849 in the Early English style at a cost of about £2000, of which £650 was raised from the various church building societies and the rest by voluntary subscriptions. It was built to cater for the people of Leftwich. It is no longer there today.

CROWTON, *The Village c1955* C481003

Crowton is a small village to the west of Weaverham. This scene shows the main road junction in the village: Kingsley Road and Station Road join here, and Ainsworth Lane comes in from the left. The attractive two-tier bellcote of Christ Church, built in 1871 to a late 13th-century design, rises above the rooftops as it does today, although the attractive half-timbered cottage in front of the church has been demolished.

DAVENHAM, *The Church from the South-West 1898* 42149

The church of St Wilfred is a large Victorian building, and is largely a reconstruction of a previous church. Tradition says that pagan Celts practised their religious rites here, and that in later years, St Wilfred established an early church during his travels through the county.

DAVENHAM
The View from the Church Tower c1955
D152003

Davenham used to be a village in its own right, but following the industrial expansion of Northwich in the late 1800s and early 1900s, its population grew until it became a residential suburb of the town. The locals would not thank you for considering them as inhabitants of Northwich, however. The scene has changed little today, but visitors are no longer allowed to appreciate it from this viewpoint, as the church tower is now closed to the public.

GREAT BUDWORTH, *The Church of St Mary and All Saints 1898* 42151

The church of St Mary and All Saints is a fine sandstone building, the oldest parts of which date from the 14th century. It dominates not only the village but much of the surrounding countryside too, and is one of the finest examples of the Perpendicular style of architecture to be found anywhere in the county.

HARTFORD
The Church
1900 45423

The fine, solid church of St John the Baptist stands at the northern end of Hartford. It was built between 1874-75 to a design by John Douglas, but a higher stair turret (visible on the left of the tower) was added in 1887-89. The church has a very interesting interior; the chancel is particularly noteworthy - it has totally different sides, and has recently been extended.

WEAVERHAM, *The Parish Church c1955* W368015

The lovely sandstone tower of St Mary's church still dominates the village today as it has since the 15th century, though a church stood here in 1086 and even much earlier. There is a rumour that excavations in the churchyard in the 1930s revealed 50 human skeletons, each with a large hole in the forehead. It is thought that the bodies may be from a mass execution that took place during the Civil War.

WHITEGATE, *The Parish Church c1960* W529037

There has been a church here since the 14th century, but the present church was re-built in the 17th century. The original church originated as a chapel for the monks during the building of Vale Royal Abbey. It became a parish church at the Dissolution. It is thought that the name 'Whitegate' stems either from the fact that it evolved outside the white gate leading to Vale Royal Abbey, or because the Cistercian monks wore white habits and were known as 'Whites'.

37

NORTHWICH'S RURAL FRINGE

MARBURY HALL *1898* 42146

This lovely building was the seat of the Barry and Smith-Barry family. It was built in the early 19th century along the lines of the French royal palace of Fontainebleau. During the Second World War it became a base for American soldiers. After standing empty for many years it was demolished in 1968, sad to say.

VALE ROYAL
1898 42147

Vale Royal house stands on the site of Vale Royal Abbey, founded in 1277 by Prince Edward, later Edward I of England, 'in honour of Mary, the Mother of God'. When completed, the planned church was due to be 420ft in length; it would have been longer than Westminster Abbey, the largest Cistercian abbey church in England and the finest abbey church in the whole of Europe. However, it was never completed.

VALE ROYAL *1898* 42148

Here we see the magnificent Victorian south front of Vale Royal, the former country seat of the Lords of Delamere. The mansion house was first built in the early part of the 17th century by Thomas Holcroft; he had the abbey church pulled down, but incorporated parts of the original abbey into the house's construction. Since then it has been extensively altered, and now houses Vale Royal Golf Club and several private apartments. Some Tudor/Jacobean timbers and walls still survive in the southern ranges.

◄ THE FLASHES
c1960 W561015

Here we see a busy scene on Bottom Flash, Winsford. There are two flashes at Winsford, Top Flash and Bottom Flash. Bottom Flash is at the end of the navigable section of the River Weaver.

◀ **NEUMAN'S FLASH** *c1960*
N43035

Neuman's Flash was named after a mine owned by a Swiss proprietor called Neuman. These small lakes are fairly common in the Northwich area, and are caused by ground subsidence due to salt extraction. The resulting depressions fill with water, creating miniature lakes, many of which have become important wildlife habitats and recreational venues.

▲ **COMBERBACH,** *The Avenue c1955* C479001

When the prisoner of war camp closed at Marbury Hall in 1918, one of the timber huts was moved to this site to act as a garage. Amazingly it is still there, virtually unchanged from the one visible in the photograph except that the Esso sign now reads Flare and the petrol pumps have been replaced by more modern versions - although the old ones are still there at the side of the garage. The Avenue runs through the northern part of the village, joining Warrington Road with Gibb Hill, and is still a quiet, leafy lane.

◀ **COMBERBACH**
The Spinner and Bergamot Inn c1955
C479011

The Spinner and Bergamot Inn has been a famous feature in the village of Comberbach since it was built. It is thought to have been named after two famous local racehorses owned by the Smith Barry family of nearby Marbury Hall (now demolished).

COMBERBACH
The War Memorial c1955 C479006

Standing next to the Memorial Hall, this sandstone monument was erected by the residents of Comberbach, Marbury and Cogshall in memory of those who lost their lives in two World Wars. The Comberbach Bowling Club now stands to the rear of the monument.

COMBERBACH, *The Memorial Hall c1955* C479007

Standing to the east of Warrington Road, this building still looks very much as it did back in the mid 1950s with its green tin roof protecting it from the elements. Recorded as 'Comburbach' in 1333, the name probably means 'stream of the Welshmen', from 'Cumbre', an Old English word for the Welsh or Gaelic people.

COMBERBACH
The Village c1955
C479014

We are looking along Warrington Road, with Willow and Park View Cottages on the left with a bicycle and an old Ford Popular parked outside. The vehicle is extinct now, but the cottages are still there, although a few structural alterations have been made.

DELAMERE, *The Forest from Ashton Road c1955* D153005

Delamere Forest is all that remains of the great Norman hunting forest of Mara, which once stretched from the River Mersey to Northwich. 'Delamere' is a French phrase meaning 'of the mere', and was given to the area by the great Norman kings following the Battle of Hastings. It refers to the many shining pools and spongy mosses that are still hidden in the depths of the forest today.

HATCHMERE, *Ashton Road c1955* H528004

Ashton Road runs through the northern fringes of the Delamere Forest. This photograph is taken looking east along the road towards the village of Hatchmere, a scene that has changed little today, apart from the style and volume of traffic passing along it.

DELAMERE, *The Jewish Fresh Air Home and School c1965* D153016

This establishment was founded by Margaret Langdon in 1920, and was known as 'The Jewish Fresh Air Home and School for Delicate Manchester and Salford Children'. It is now the Delamere Forest School. The open-air and 'back to nature' educational movements so prevalent in the first decades of the 20th century, were primarily concerned with the healthy body and healthy mind. The school catered for children suffering from malnutrition, domestic squalor and maladjustment.

HATCHMERE
The Forest Café c1955
H528034

The Forest café and ice cream parlour stood at the junction of Ashton Road and Delamere Road in Hatchmere until December 2002, when it was demolished to make way for a new housing development. It was a very popular venue for cyclists and walkers, and it was obviously trying to attract the attention of those with a sweet tooth back in the 1950s with its left-hand window display full of jars of goodies. The billboards outside sound out the newspaper headlines of the time. The Sunday Mirror – 'The world of the formerly married'. The News of the World – 'Ulysses: the inside story of the film'. The People – 'Debs! The truth at last – by the man who knows'. The Sunday Express – '1,000 hours of hell'. Times change, but newspapers and their headlines remain much the same.

SAILING DINGHIES ON BUDWORTH MERE *c1960* N43041

Budworth Mere has been a popular venue for sailing, angling and bird watching for many years. It is now part of Marbury Country Park, which was formed from the parkland, grounds and gardens that once belonged to Marbury Hall.

BUDWORTH MERE
c1960 N43038

This nostalgic scene shows sheaves of corn stacked to dry in the fields surrounding Budworth Mere. In the middle ages the mere was used as a fish hatchery to supply nearby streams and ponds. The stocks of fish are still plentiful, and provide good sport for anglers.

GREAT BUDWORTH, *The Village 1898* 42152

This photograph is taken looking east along Great Budworth's High Street. The village contains all the elements that one would expect of an attractive settlement with appealing cottages nestling in the shadow of its mighty church. Note the partly cobbled pavements and the range of architectural styles in the buildings and boundary walls, reflecting the 17th-century, Georgian and Victorian styles.

THE TOWNS AND VILLAGES AROUND NORTHWICH

CROWTON, *Kingsley Road c1955* C481013

We are looking east. The shop on the right of the road was Crowton post office, now closed, and the building attached to it is now extended, rendered and aptly named The Old Post Office. Long ago this village lay within the bounds of the forest of Mara.

CUDDINGTON
Mere Lane,
The New Estate
c1960 C435014

This range of buildings in Mere Lane still looks much as it did in the 1960s, though the shops have changed trades several times and now comprise a hair salon, a fruit and vegetable shop, a butcher's, a newsagent's and a chip shop. The name Mere Lane denotes the existence of meres hereabouts.

CUDDINGTON, *The White Barn Hotel c1955* C435017

The White Barn Hotel stands at the cross-roads between the A49 Warrington Road and Norley Road. Cuddington lies on the line of the old Roman road; its name derives from the early Saxon, and means 'the village of the people of Cudda', which may perhaps suggest the existence of an early village site.

▼ **CUDDINGTON,** *Cartledge Close c1960* C435018

Cuddington is an amalgamation of two villages, Cuddington itself and Sandiway, both of which had existed as separate settlements until 1935. Since then they have blended together to form a large and thriving community.

► **CUDDINGTON**
The Post Office c1965
C435052

Cuddington Post Office (right), in Trickett Lane, still trades today, though the vehicles that pull up outside today are a little more modern.

◀ DAVENHAM
The Village c1965
D152019

Apart from a few coats of paint and the changes in retailers, this scene looking along Church Street from London Road has changed little. The Burt Price cycle and electrical shop (left) is now Davenham Pharmacy, Poole's Radio and TV shop (right) is now a dress shop, and Greenall Whitley's off licence along Church Street (centre) is a restaurant.

▶ DAVENHAM
The War Memorial and the School c1955
D152001

Davenham Church of England Primary School no longer has throngs of youngsters passing through its doors - it is now converted into several private residences. But despite that, the building looks much as it did in this photograph. The trees that flank the war memorial are a little taller, and the young man sitting on the wall (centre) has moved on and grown up. I wonder if he was wagging lessons?

▶ **DAVENHAM**
The Roundabout
c1955 D152011

This roundabout at the junction of London Road and the A556 is still there, but it is a much busier intersection today than the one we see here. On the other side of the roundabout is Leftwich. The large, gable-ended dwelling on the left has now gone to make way for a new housing development, and the building across the roundabout, which used to be a magistrate's home, is now a hotel.

◀ **GREAT BUDWORTH**
School Lane c1965
G201005

These 17th-century timber-framed cottages, which overlook the churchyard, still look very similar today. The cobbled School Lane leads past Great Budworth C of E Primary School and down to a lovely avenue of mature trees, through which there are fine glimpses across the Cheshire Plain.

▲ **GREAT BUDWORTH,** *High Street c1965* G201008

The George and Dragon Inn sits right in the centre of the village and directly opposite the church. There used to be three other alehouses in the village in the past - the White Hart, the Ring o' Bells and the Saracen's Head - but these have now been converted to private dwellings. The ornate wrought iron sign hanging out from the inn was specially made in Germany.

◀**GREAT BUDWORTH** *An Old Cottage, Church Street c1965* G201009

This lovely old cottage, No 43 Church Street, is typical of many cottages in the village, with its black, half-timbered square frame and white-painted infill. The charm and character of this delightfully informal village stems from the fact that it was largely owned by the Egerton-Warburton family from nearby Arley Hall. They commissioned distinguished Victorian architects to restore a number of the houses and to build others in a sympathetic style.

◄**SANDIWAY**
*The Round Tower,
c1940* S490008

The Round Tower at
Sandiway, in Cuddington
is now all that remains of a
gatehouse to Lord
Delamere's Vale Royal
House. Unfortunately,
despite some renovation
in recent years, the tower
now stands bang in the
middle of the A559 dual
carriageway. The road in
the picture now carries
east-bound traffic towards
Northwich, while a new
road on the opposite side
of the tower carries west-
bound traffic.

◄ **HARTFORD**
Whitehall,
School Lane
1940 H323003

Hartford Lodge, now known as Whitehall, was once occupied by a family called Deakin. Legend goes that they caught the infamous criminal Charles Peace attempting to rob Hartford Lodge, so they bricked him up in a wall in the house. His body is still supposed to be there. Whitehall is now used by Hartford Business Centre.

▲ **HARTFORD,** *The Cross Roads c1955* H323018

Hartford stands on the site of a ford across the nearby River Weaver. With the coming of the Romans, the ford grew in importance, and it was used by the Roman Watling Street. It must have seen quite regular traffic with salt traders and Roman soldiers passing between the Delamere Forest and Castle, the site of the Roman fort in Condate (Northwich). The cross-roads form the junction of the A556 Northwich-Chester Road, Bradburns Lane and School Lane.

◄ **HARTFORD**
School Lane c1955
H323023

During the Industrial Revolution, wealthy local manufacturers chose to make their homes in rural Hartford. With the coming of Brunner Mond (later ICI) to nearby Winnington in 1873, the rural nature of the village began to change: the population expanded, and housing developments such as these along School Lane were constructed. The grass verges still front the properties today, but the road is now a busy thoroughfare through Hartford.

HARTFORD, *The Bridge 1940* H323002

Hartford Bridge carries the A556 dual carriageway high above the River Weaver. This picture looks east, with Leftwich and Davenham on the sky-line. The scene has changed little since this photograph was taken, except for the volume and nature of the traffic on the road.

WEAVERHAM
High Street c1955 W368002

Little has actually changed here over the years, apart from the names and trades of the various shops – and, of course, the modes of transport. Buckley's (right) is now a Cosy Warm Heating shop. The building to its left now has a thatched roof, and the white building beyond with the window cleaners busy at work is now Cohen's Chemists. The Wheatsheaf Inn on the left still trades under its original name, but live football on the tv has replaced dominoes and darts.

WEAVERHAM, *The Village c1955* W368019

Here we have an almost traffic-free view along the High Street. The telephone box is no longer there, and H Garner & Son's butcher's shop to its right is now a wine bar. The sign for Will's Capstan full strength cigarettes above Hornby's Store (right, now a hair salon) is something that you will not see today.

▼ **WEAVERHAM,** *The Post Office, Lime Avenue c1955* W368013

This range of shops in Lime Avenue still serves the surrounding housing estate, and apart from the window displays and the names of the retailers, little has changed. The post office has gone to be replaced by a wine store and a Chinese take-away.

► **WEAVERHAM**
The Gate Inn c1965
W368029

Traces of a Roman road have been excavated in the middle of Weaverham; in medieval times the road was known as Poitevins Way or Peytefynsty. This ancient route divided the forests of Mara and Mondrem; Mara lay to the north and west, and Mondrem to the south and east.

◀ **WHITEGATE**
Cinder Hill c1960
W529038

Whitegate was the estate village for the Lords of Delamere, who had their family seat at nearby Vale Royal. In early medieval times this settlement was known as Conewardsley, but it was depopulated to make way for the monastery. The white building on the left, White Gate House, used to be the Rifleman Inn.

▶ **WINSFORD**
Fountain Court
c1965 W561046

Winsford takes its name from an old ford over the River Weaver, but as a settlement it is more modern than ancient. A massive redevelopment programme in the 1960s and 70s virtually obliterated the old town centre, turning it into a modern, largely undercover, shopping precinct. The fountain has gone, and is now replaced by two war memorials.

WINSFORD
The Post Office c1955
W561003

We are looking along the High Street. The road is still there, but many of the buildings have been demolished, and a new dual carriageway now carries traffic through the town. The post office building (right) still stands at the time of writing; it was last trading as the Lighthouse fish and chip shop.

THE WEAVER NAVIGATION

THE VIADUCT *1898* 42143

This impressive structure, built in the early 1860s, is over 1,000 yards long and consists of 48 arches and two iron girder spans (visible in the photograph). It crosses three water courses: the River Dane, the old course of the River Weaver and the man-made Weaver Navigation.

THE VIADUCT AND HUNT'S LOCKS
1898 42144

Hunt's Locks stand on the site of one of the original eleven locks built by the Weaver Navigation Trust. In the late 1800s they were doubled up to allow two-way traffic and so speed up the movement of barges along the navigation.

THE VIADUCT *1898* 42145

One of the many sailing barges that traded along the Weaver is tied up outside Hunt's Locks. The two metal girder spans in the railway viaduct could be removed if necessary to allow the tall-masted ocean-going vessels to pass along the navigation.

HUNT'S LOCKS *c1955* N43024

▼ VALE ROYAL VIADUCT *1898* 42148a

This photograph, taken from the south, shows the railway viaduct and a footbridge spanning the River Weaver at Vale Royal Locks. This is where a natural section of the river remains, but with a canalised section running parallel to it.

▶ VALE ROYAL VIADUCT *c1955* D152009

The Vale Royal Viaduct with its solid, symmetrical arches, one of the earliest of its type on the railways, was built to carry the London to Glasgow west coast line over the River Weaver. It was the inspiration of George Stephenson (of Rocket fame), but being a mechanical rather than a civil engineer, he turned to Joseph Lock to assist him with his idea for the span.

◀ **TOWN BRIDGE**
c1965 N43063

Town Bridge was originally a stone bridge and an early crossing point over the River Weaver. In medieval times the bridge was often thrown down by flood waters, and a regular ferry service conveyed people across the river.

▶ **HAYHURST BRIDGE** *c1960*
N43031

Hayhurst Bridge and Town Bridge, built in 1898 and 1899 respectively, are believed to be the first electrically powered swing bridges in Britain, and the first to be built on floating pontoons. Both of these initiatives came about because of subsidence due to salt extraction; electric cables, unlike pipes, bend rather than break when the ground gives way, and a floating pivot is totally unaffected by subsidence. The idea of building two bridges also meant that road traffic could always enter or leave the town when one or other's structure was swung open to allow a ship to pass.

THE SWING BRIDGE
1900 45422

This shows Town Bridge just
one year after it was
constructed in 1899; we are
looking west towards
Winnington Street. The
gentleman on the left of the
picture wearing a peaked
cap was the bridge operator.

TOWN BRIDGE *c1960*
N43032

This shows the bridge open in order to let the motor vessel pass along the Weaver. Notice the basket on the pole attached to the bridge parapet. The basket was raised to indicate when the bridge was swung open and lowered when it was closed.

THE ANDERTON
BOAT LIFT *c1960*
N43026

This is a fine example of
Victorian engineering and
ingenuity, which became
known as 'the wonder of the
waterways'. It was
constructed so that boats
could switch from the River
Weaver to the Trent &
Mersey Canal, just 50ft
above the river and running
parallel to it. Originally the
lift operated on a hydraulic
system with two counter-
balanced water-tight tanks
raising and lowering boats
between the two waterways.
The two tanks embodied in
the lift, each containing 252
tons of water, were
originally raised and
lowered by a system of
hydraulic rams, but in 1908
it was electrified so that the
tanks could be operated
independently. Despite the
fact that some 570 tons of
water and metal were
moved when the lift was
operated, the whole system
was powered by a tiny 30
horsepower electric motor.
The lift worked well until
1983, when severe corrosion
of the main support legs
forced British Waterways to
shut it down. A renovation
programme has now
returned the lift to full
working order, and people
can now take a trip on the
lift and visit the nearby
Visitor Centre.

THE RIVER *c1960* N43019

One of the many small works that once lined the banks of the River Weaver in Northwich is making use of the navigation's transport facilities. Notice the crane operating off the boat at the wharf. Health and safety would go ballistic with such a system today.

THE RIVER WEAVER
c1955 N43011

The steam packet 'Cambria', with another barge in tow, sails along the river Weaver at Winnington. This was a common sight on the navigation, with vessels like the 'Cambria' capable of towing several barges at once.

WINNINGTON BRIDGE *c1955* N43016

Winnington Bridge swings open to allow the 'Cambria' access along the Weaver Navigation. In 1659 the last battle of the English Civil War took place here when the Royalists, lead by Sir George Booth, were defeated by a detachment of Cromwell's New Model Army, commanded by General Lambert.

WINNINGTON
*The ICI Chemical
Works, c1955* N43023

This photograph shows the
wharf alongside ICI's
chemical plant (formerly
Brunner Mond) at
Winnington. The vessel on
the left has 'Imperial
Chemical Industries
Limited' painted across its
stern and is registered in
Liverpool, while the ship to
the right is the 'Wimborne',
registered in Poole.

THE RIVER *from Winnington Bridge c1955* N43022

Here we see the ICI chemical works at Winnington. A plant was established here in 1873 by John Brunner and Ludwig Mond to produce soda ash from salt. In 1926 they merged with several other companies to form the chemical giant Imperial Chemical Industries Limited (ICI).

ACTON BRIDGE
The River Weaver
c1965 A235032

The marina at Acton Bridge has always been a popular and busy place, with boats needing moorings, repairs and fuel. It is also home of the Acton Bridge Cruising Club, and their logo - ABCC – is visible on notice-boards and some of the boats.

ACTON, *The River Weaver near Acton Swing Bridge c1955* A235011

The new bridge spanning the River Weaver here at Acton was built in 1932 on a floating pontoon. Notice the extensive presence of wooden hulls. This was because of the likelihood of corrosion from salt with steel-hulled vessels.

THE RIVER WEAVER
c1960 N43059

The River Weaver has played an important role in the development of the salt industry in Northwich. Prior to 1721, it was a shallow waterway that flowed serenely from its source in the Peckforton Hills through the settlements of Wrenbury, Audlem, Nantwich, Winsford, Northwich and finally Frodsham before pouring into the saline waters of the River Mersey.

THE RIVER WEAVER
c1965 N43072

This photograph shows British Waterways' Hayhurst Bridge boat yard. By 1732 the course of the river had been straightened out, the channel deepened, and a series of locks built that could accommodate cargo boats of 100 tons. Northwich became an inland port, and boat yards sprang up along the river frontage with a wide variety of river and coastal vessels being constructed, including Weaver flats, which were flat-bottomed sailing barges.

BARNTON, *The Tunnel c1955* B518006

Here we see the entrance to the canal tunnel at Barnton on the Trent and Mersey Canal. When the canal was built, the Trustees of the Weaver Navigation were understandably extremely worried that the canal was likely to remove trade from the navigation. As it happened, a very amicable working relationship developed between the two waterways.

INDEX

Frith Book Co Titles

www.francisfrith.co.uk

The Frith Book Company publishes over 100 new titles each year. A selection of those currently available is listed below. For latest catalogue please contact Frith Book Co.
Town Books 96 pages, approximately 100 photos. **County and Themed Books** 128 pages, approximately 150 photos (unless specified). All titles hardback with laminated case and jacket, except those indicated pb (paperback)

Title	ISBN	Price	Title	ISBN	Price
Amersham, Chesham & Rickmansworth (pb)	1-85937-340-2	£9.99	Devon (pb)	1-85937-297-x	£9.99
Andover (pb)	1-85937-292-9	£9.99	Devon Churches (pb)	1-85937-250-3	£9.99
Aylesbury (pb)	1-85937-227-9	£9.99	Dorchester (pb)	1-85937-307-0	£9.99
Barnstaple (pb)	1-85937-300-3	£9.99	Dorset (pb)	1-85937-269-4	£9.99
Basildon Living Memories (pb)	1-85937-515-4	£9.99	Dorset Coast (pb)	1-85937-299-6	£9.99
Bath (pb)	1-85937-419-0	£9.99	Dorset Living Memories (pb)	1-85937-584-7	£9.99
Bedford (pb)	1-85937-205-8	£9.99	Down the Severn (pb)	1-85937-560-x	£9.99
Bedfordshire Living Memories	1-85937-513-8	£14.99	Down The Thames (pb)	1-85937-278-3	£9.99
Belfast (pb)	1-85937-303-8	£9.99	Down the Trent	1-85937-311-9	£14.99
Berkshire (pb)	1-85937-191-4	£9.99	East Anglia (pb)	1-85937-265-1	£9.99
Berkshire Churches	1-85937-170-1	£17.99	East Grinstead (pb)	1-85937-138-8	£9.99
Berkshire Living Memories	1-85937-332-1	£14.99	East London	1-85937-080-2	£14.99
Black Country	1-85937-497-2	£12.99	East Sussex (pb)	1-85937-606-1	£9.99
Blackpool (pb)	1-85937-393-3	£9.99	Eastbourne (pb)	1-85937-399-2	£9.99
Bognor Regis (pb)	1-85937-431-x	£9.99	Edinburgh (pb)	1-85937-193-0	£8.99
Bournemouth (pb)	1-85937-545-6	£9.99	England In The 1880s	1-85937-331-3	£17.99
Bradford (pb)	1-85937-204-x	£9.99	Essex - Second Selection	1-85937-456-5	£14.99
Bridgend (pb)	1-85937-386-0	£7.99	Essex (pb)	1-85937-270-8	£9.99
Bridgwater (pb)	1-85937-305-4	£9.99	Essex Coast	1-85937-342-9	£14.99
Bridport (pb)	1-85937-327-5	£9.99	Essex Living Memories	1-85937-490-5	£14.99
Brighton (pb)	1-85937-192-2	£8.99	Exeter	1-85937-539-1	£9.99
Bristol (pb)	1-85937-264-3	£9.99	Exmoor (pb)	1-85937-608-8	£9.99
British Life A Century Ago (pb)	1-85937-213-9	£9.99	Falmouth (pb)	1-85937-594-4	£9.99
Buckinghamshire (pb)	1-85937-200-7	£9.99	Folkestone (pb)	1-85937-124-8	£9.99
Camberley (pb)	1-85937-222-8	£9.99	Frome (pb)	1-85937-317-8	£9.99
Cambridge (pb)	1-85937-422-0	£9.99	Glamorgan	1-85937-488-3	£14.99
Cambridgeshire (pb)	1-85937-420-4	£9.99	Glasgow (pb)	1-85937-190-6	£9.99
Cambridgeshire Villages	1-85937-523-5	£14.99	Glastonbury (pb)	1-85937-338-0	£7.99
Canals And Waterways (pb)	1-85937-291-0	£9.99	Gloucester (pb)	1-85937-232-5	£9.99
Canterbury Cathedral (pb)	1-85937-179-5	£9.99	Gloucestershire (pb)	1-85937-561-8	£9.99
Cardiff (pb)	1-85937-093-4	£9.99	Great Yarmouth (pb)	1-85937-426-3	£9.99
Carmarthenshire (pb)	1-85937-604-5	£9.99	Greater Manchester (pb)	1-85937-266-x	£9.99
Chelmsford (pb)	1-85937-310-0	£9.99	Guildford (pb)	1-85937-410-7	£9.99
Cheltenham (pb)	1-85937-095-0	£9.99	Hampshire (pb)	1-85937-279-1	£9.99
Cheshire (pb)	1-85937-271-6	£9.99	Harrogate (pb)	1-85937-423-9	£9.99
Chester (pb)	1-85937-382 8	£9.99	Hastings and Bexhill (pb)	1-85937-131-0	£9.99
Chesterfield (pb)	1-85937-378-x	£9.99	Heart of Lancashire (pb)	1-85937-197-3	£9.99
Chichester (pb)	1-85937-228-7	£9.99	Helston (pb)	1-85937-214-7	£9.99
Churches of East Cornwall (pb)	1-85937-249-x	£9.99	Hereford (pb)	1-85937-175-2	£9.99
Churches of Hampshire (pb)	1-85937-207-4	£9.99	Herefordshire (pb)	1-85937-567-7	£9.99
Cinque Ports & Two Ancient Towns	1-85937-492-1	£14.99	Herefordshire Living Memories	1-85937-514-6	£14.99
Colchester (pb)	1-85937-188-4	£8.99	Hertfordshire (pb)	1-85937-247-3	£9.99
Cornwall (pb)	1-85937-229-5	£9.99	Horsham (pb)	1-85937-432-8	£9.99
Cornwall Living Memories	1-85937-248-1	£14.99	Humberside (pb)	1-85937-605-3	£9.99
Cotswolds (pb)	1-85937-230-9	£9.99	Hythe, Romney Marsh, Ashford (pb)	1-85937-256-2	£9.99
Cotswolds Living Memories	1-85937-255-4	£14.99	Ipswich (pb)	1-85937-424-7	£9.99
County Durham (pb)	1-85937-398-4	£9.99	Isle of Man (pb)	1-85937-268-6	£9.99
Croydon Living Memories (pb)	1-85937-162-0	£9.99	Isle of Wight (pb)	1-85937-429-8	£9.99
Cumbria (pb)	1-85937-621-5	£9.99	Isle of Wight Living Memories	1-85937-304-6	£14.99
Derby (pb)	1-85937-367-4	£9.99	Kent (pb)	1-85937-189-2	£9.99
Derbyshire (pb)	1-85937-196-5	£9.99	Kent Living Memories(pb)	1-85937-401-8	£9.99
Derbyshire Living Memories	1-85937-330-5	£14.99	Kings Lynn (pb)	1-85937-334-8	£9.99

Available from your local bookshop or from the publisher

Frith Book Co Titles (continued)

Lake District (pb)	1-85937-275-9	£9.99	Sherborne (pb)	1-85937-301-1	£9.99
Lancashire Living Memories	1-85937-335-6	£14.99	Shrewsbury (pb)	1-85937-325-9	£9.99
Lancaster, Morecambe, Heysham (pb)	1-85937-233-3	£9.99	Shropshire (pb)	1-85937-326-7	£9.99
Leeds (pb)	1-85937-202-3	£9.99	Shropshire Living Memories	1-85937-643-6	£14.99
Leicester (pb)	1-85937-381-x	£9.99	Somerset	1-85937-153-1	£14.99
Leicestershire & Rutland Living Memories	1-85937-500-6	£12.99	South Devon Coast	1-85937-107-8	£14.99
Leicestershire (pb)	1-85937-185-x	£9.99	South Devon Living Memories (pb)	1-85937-609-6	£9.99
Lighthouses	1-85937-257-0	£9.99	South East London (pb)	1-85937-263-5	£9.99
Lincoln (pb)	1-85937-380-1	£9.99	South Somerset	1-85937-318-6	£14.99
Lincolnshire (pb)	1-85937-433-6	£9.99	South Wales	1-85937-519-7	£14.99
Liverpool and Merseyside (pb)	1-85937-234-1	£9.99	Southampton (pb)	1-85937-427-1	£9.99
London (pb)	1-85937-183-3	£9.99	Southend (pb)	1-85937-313-5	£9.99
London Living Memories	1-85937-454-9	£14.99	Southport (pb)	1-85937-425-5	£9.99
Ludlow (pb)	1-85937-176-0	£9.99	St Albans (pb)	1-85937-341-0	£9.99
Luton (pb)	1-85937-235-x	£9.99	St Ives (pb)	1-85937-415-8	£9.99
Maidenhead (pb)	1-85937-339-9	£9.99	Stafford Living Memories (pb)	1-85937-503-0	£9.99
Maidstone (pb)	1-85937-391-7	£9.99	Staffordshire (pb)	1-85937-308-9	£9.99
Manchester (pb)	1-85937-198-1	£9.99	Stourbridge (pb)	1-85937-530-8	£9.99
Marlborough (pb)	1-85937-336-4	£9.99	Stratford upon Avon (pb)	1-85937-388-7	£9.99
Middlesex	1-85937-158-2	£14.99	Suffolk (pb)	1-85937-221-x	£9.99
Monmouthshire	1-85937-532-4	£14.99	Suffolk Coast (pb)	1-85937-610-x	£9.99
New Forest (pb)	1-85937-390-9	£9.99	Surrey (pb)	1-85937-240-6	£9.99
Newark (pb)	1-85937-366-6	£9.99	Surrey Living Memories	1-85937-328-3	£14.99
Newport, Wales (pb)	1-85937-258-9	£9.99	Sussex (pb)	1-85937-184-1	£9.99
Newquay (pb)	1-85937-421-2	£9.99	Sutton (pb)	1-85937-337-2	£9.99
Norfolk (pb)	1-85937-195-7	£9.99	Swansea (pb)	1-85937-167-1	£9.99
Norfolk Broads	1-85937-486-7	£14.99	Taunton (pb)	1-85937-314-3	£9.99
Norfolk Living Memories (pb)	1-85937-402-6	£9.99	Tees Valley & Cleveland (pb)	1-85937-623-1	£9.99
North Buckinghamshire	1-85937-626-6	£14.99	Teignmouth (pb)	1-85937-370-4	£7.99
North Devon Living Memories	1-85937-261-9	£14.99	Thanet (pb)	1-85937-116-7	£9.99
North Hertfordshire	1-85937-547-2	£14.99	Tiverton (pb)	1-85937-178-7	£9.99
North London (pb)	1-85937-403-4	£9.99	Torbay (pb)	1-85937-597-9	£9.99
North Somerset	1-85937-302-x	£14.99	Truro (pb)	1-85937-598-7	£9.99
North Wales (pb)	1-85937-298-8	£9.99	Victorian & Edwardian Dorset	1-85937-254-6	£14.99
North Yorkshire (pb)	1-85937-236-8	£9.99	Victorian & Edwardian Kent (pb)	1-85937-624-X	£9.99
Northamptonshire Living Memories	1-85937-529-4	£14.99	Victorian & Edwardian Maritime Album (pb)	1-85937-622-3	£9.99
Northamptonshire	1-85937-150-7	£14.99	Victorian and Edwardian Sussex (pb)	1-85937-625-8	£9.99
Northumberland Tyne & Wear (pb)	1-85937-281-3	£9.99	Villages of Devon (pb)	1-85937-293-7	£9.99
Northumberland	1-85937-522-7	£14.99	Villages of Kent (pb)	1-85937-294-5	£9.99
Norwich (pb)	1-85937-194-9	£8.99	Villages of Sussex (pb)	1-85937-295-3	£9.99
Nottingham (pb)	1-85937-324-0	£9.99	Warrington (pb)	1-85937-507-3	£9.99
Nottinghamshire (pb)	1-85937-187-6	£9.99	Warwick (pb)	1-85937-518-9	£9.99
Oxford (pb)	1-85937-411-5	£9.99	Warwickshire (pb)	1-85937-203-1	£9.99
Oxfordshire (pb)	1-85937-430-1	£9.99	Welsh Castles (pb)	1-85937-322-4	£9.99
Oxfordshire Living Memories	1-85937-525-1	£14.99	West Midlands (pb)	1-85937-289-9	£9.99
Paignton (pb)	1-85937-374-7	£7.99	West Sussex (pb)	1-85937-607-x	£9.99
Peak District (pb)	1-85937-280-5	£9.99	West Yorkshire (pb)	1-85937-201-5	£9.99
Pembrokeshire	1-85937-262-7	£14.99	Weston Super Mare (pb)	1-85937-306-2	£9.99
Penzance (pb)	1-85937-595-2	£9.99	Weymouth (pb)	1-85937-209-0	£9.99
Peterborough (pb)	1-85937-219-8	£9.99	Wiltshire (pb)	1-85937-277-5	£9.99
Picturesque Harbours	1-85937-208-2	£14.99	Wiltshire Churches (pb)	1-85937-171-x	£9.99
Piers	1-85937-237-6	£17.99	Wiltshire Living Memories (pb)	1-85937-396-8	£9.99
Plymouth (pb)	1-85937-389-5	£9.99	Winchester (pb)	1-85937-428-x	£9.99
Poole & Sandbanks (pb)	1-85937-251-1	£9.99	Windsor (pb)	1-85937-333-x	£9.99
Preston (pb)	1-85937-212-0	£9.99	Wokingham & Bracknell (pb)	1-85937-329-1	£9.99
Reading (pb)	1-85937-238-4	£9.99	Woodbridge (pb)	1-85937-498-0	£9.99
Redhill to Reigate (pb)	1-85937-596-0	£9.99	Worcester (pb)	1-85937-165-5	£9.99
Ringwood (pb)	1-85937-384-4	£7.99	Worcestershire Living Memories	1-85937-489-1	£14.99
Romford (pb)	1-85937-319-4	£9.99	Worcestershire	1-85937-152-3	£14.99
Royal Tunbridge Wells (pb)	1-85937-504-9	£9.99	York (pb)	1-85937-199-x	£9.99
Salisbury (pb)	1-85937-239-2	£9.99	Yorkshire (pb)	1-85937-186-8	£9.99
Scarborough (pb)	1-85937-379-8	£9.99	Yorkshire Coastal Memories	1-85937-506-5	£14.99
Sevenoaks and Tonbridge (pb)	1-85937-392-5	£9.99	Yorkshire Dales	1-85937-502-2	£14.99
Sheffield & South Yorks (pb)	1-85937-267-8	£9.99	Yorkshire Living Memories (pb)	1-85937-397-6	£9.99

See Frith books on the internet at www.francisfrith.co.uk

FRITH PRODUCTS & SERVICES

Francis Frith would doubtless be pleased to know that the pioneering publishing venture he started in 1860 still continues today. Over a hundred and forty years later, The Francis Frith Collection continues in the same innovative tradition and is now one of the foremost publishers of vintage photographs in the world. Some of the current activities include:

Interior Decoration

Today Frith's photographs can be seen framed and as giant wall murals in thousands of pubs, restaurants, hotels, banks, retail stores and other public buildings throughout the country. In every case they enhance the unique local atmosphere of the places they depict and provide reminders of gentler days in an increasingly busy and frenetic world.

Product Promotions

Frith products are used by many major companies to promote the sales of their own products or to reinforce their own history and heritage. Frith promotions have been used by Hovis bread, Courage beers, Scots Porage Oats, Colman's mustard, Cadbury's foods, Mellow Birds coffee, Dunhill pipe tobacco, Guinness, and Bulmer's Cider.

Genealogy and Family History

As the interest in family history and roots grows world-wide, more and more people are turning to Frith's photographs of Great Britain for images of the towns, villages and streets where their ancestors lived; and, of course, photographs of the churches and chapels where their ancestors were christened, married and buried are an essential part of every genealogy tree and family album.

Frith Products

All Frith photographs are available Framed or just as Mounted Prints and Posters (size 23 x 16 inches). These may be ordered from the address below. From time to time other products - Address Books, Calendars, Table Mats, etc - are available.

The Internet

Already fifty thousand Frith photographs can be viewed and purchased on the internet through the Frith websites and a myriad of partner sites.

For more detailed information on Frith companies and products, look at these sites:

www.francisfrith.co.uk
www.francisfrith.com
(for North American visitors)

See the complete list of Frith Books at:

www.francisfrith.co.uk

This web site is regularly updated with the latest list of publications from the Frith Book Company. If you wish to buy books relating to another part of the country that your local bookshop does not stock, you may purchase on-line.

For further information, trade, or author enquiries please contact us at the address below:
The Francis Frith Collection, Frith's Barn, Teffont, Salisbury, Wiltshire, England SP3 5QP.
Tel: +44 (0)1722 716 376 Fax: +44 (0)1722 716 881 Email: sales@francisfrith.co.uk

See Frith books on the internet at www.francisfrith.co.uk

FREE MOUNTED PRINT

Mounted Print
Overall size 14 x 11 inches

Fill in and cut out this voucher and return
it with your remittance for £2.25 (to cover postage and handling). Offer valid for delivery to UK addresses only.

Choose any photograph included in this book.
Your SEPIA print will be A4 in size. It will be mounted in a cream mount with a burgundy rule line (overall size 14 x 11 inches).

**Order additional Mounted Prints
at HALF PRICE (only £7.49 each*)**
If you would like to order more Frith prints from this book, possibly as gifts for friends and family, you can buy them at half price (with no additional postage and handling costs).

Have your Mounted Prints framed
For an extra £14.95 per print* you can have your mounted print(s) framed in an elegant polished wood and gilt moulding, overall size 16 x 13 inches (no additional postage and handling required).

---

* IMPORTANT!

These special prices are only available if you order at the same time as you order your free mounted print. You must use the ORIGINAL VOUCHER on this page (no copies permitted). We can only despatch to one address.

Send completed Voucher form to:
The Francis Frith Collection, Frith's Barn, Teffont, Salisbury, Wiltshire SP3 5QP